National
Restaurant News

RESTAURANT MANAGER'S POCKET HANDBOOK

FOOD COST

25 KEYS TO

Profitable
Success

DAVID V. PAVESIC, F.M.P.

Copyright© 1999 by David V. Pavesic, Ph.D.
Lebhar-Friedman Books

Lebhar-Friedman Books is a company of Lebhar-Friedman Inc.

Printed in the United States of America

Library of Congress Cataloging-in-Publication Data

Pavesic, David V.
    Restaurant manager's pocket handbook : 25 keys to
profitable success. Food cost / David V. Pavesic.
       p. cm.
    Includes index.
    ISBN 0-86730-755-2 (pbk.)
    1. Food service--Cost control. I. Title.
TX911.3.C65P385 1998
647.95'0681--dc21   98-39301
                                   CIP

AS PROFESSIONALS in the restaurant industry, we must have a more in-depth understanding of the factors that impact the operational efficiency of our business. Because the objective of being in this business in the first place is to prepare and serve food to the public at a profit, the way we view and interpret food cost should be rigorous and complete. It cannot be regarded as a one-dimensional ratio or concept; it must be viewed from four different perspectives.

Expenditures for food represent the largest expense borne by a foodservice operation. That fact alone justifies the detail and attention accorded food-cost control. You simply cannot adopt a competitor's food cost or apply an industry average to your operation. Each operation will differ slightly from another, and even if by some chance two were identical, the resulting bottom-line profit percentage wouldn't be the same.

There are hundreds of reasons why food costs might not meet cost standards — reasons that encompass the entire range of business activities in both the front- and back-of-the-house. One cannot automatically assume that the causes for high food cost are the fault of the kitchen and ignore what is taking place in the dining room. The problems driving high food cost could be in place even before the food is delivered to the restaurant. If any weakness exists within the entire cycle of ordering, receiving, storage, preparation, service, cash receipts, and accounts payable, your food costs might not be so low as they could be.

This book offers insights into areas that could impact your food cost. If some hit a nerve, you probably will be compelled to review your practices and make the necessary changes to bring your food costs in line. Remember: The first step in correcting a problem is recognizing that you have one. Once you've discovered the problem, you can prevent it from occurring again.

Embrace food cost, not as a single percentage, but from four different perspectives

AS A FOODSERVICE PROFESSIONAL, you must examine food cost in far greater detail and depth than perhaps you ever have realized. The more you understand it, the greater will be your ability to interpret and control it. Being able to calculate or compute food cost does not in itself reflect an understanding of its importance. The majority of foodservice workers consider food cost a one-dimensional ratio calculated by dividing cost of food by food sales. But that definition is equivocal and incomplete.

To be able to appreciate the full value of food-cost control, it must be examined from what I term "the four faces of food cost." Those four faces, or perspectives, are *maximum allowable, actual, potential,* and *standard.* For more on the concepts, see *25 Keys to Profitable Success: Cost Controls.*

> **"Good business leaders create a vision, articulate the vision, passionately own the vision, and relentlessly drive it to completion."**
>
> — JOHN WELCH

Food-cost percentage is often misused and its importance understated. Calculating a monthly food cost is irrelevant if a fiscal inventory is not taken at the end of the accounting period. A calculated food-cost percentage doesn't reveal if it is a good or bad number if it's not compared with a standard. Setting a standard food-cost percentage cannot be accomplished by using an industry average.

Assume that you're opening a new restaurant and preparing a pro-forma income statement. What percentage of food cost should you run? The answer to that question is answered partially by the calculation of the *maximum allowable food-cost percentage*, or MFC. The MFC is different for just about every restaurant — even for the same type of units offering the same menu. The reason is that each unit has its own financial idiosyncrasies. By that I mean the capital investment and operating costs won't be exactly the same for any two units in a restaurant chain. Land, rent, taxes, interest, insurance, and construction costs rarely are identical.

The MFC is calculated from a pro-forma budget for which you estimate your fixed and variable operating expenses, payroll, and related taxes and then impute a minimum profit expectation. You must express your expenses and minimum profit in absolute dollar amounts. The only expense left out of your pro forma is food cost. Next, you project your sales for the same period of time reflected in your expenses. What you then have is a pro-forma income statement with every line filled in except the line opposite food cost. In essence, you have an equation that reads, "total cost without food plus profit equals 100 percent." Therefore, food cost can be calculated by subtracting total costs and profit from total sales. That dollar value divided by food sales equals your maximum allowable food-cost percentage. The MFC is the high-water mark for your food cost; if it exceeds that percentage of sales, your profit will be diminished by that percentage amount. Remember: Each operation will have its own unique MFC because it has unique expenses and sales.

The second food cost is the percentage that appears on your monthly income statement. It is a reflection of the food cost you actually ran during that accounting period, thus the name *actual food-cost percentage*, or AFC. That figure is calculated by dividing food cost by food sales. If you're following the *Uniform System of Accounts for Restaurants*, seventh edition, you will have deducted an allowance for employee meals and, in essence, have calculated cost of food sold. If you don't deduct for employee meals, you are calculating cost of food *consumed*. That is an important distinction and is explained later in key number 13. While that percentage will be lower than the MFC, one can't say if it's good or bad because there's no way of knowing at this point what it should be.

The *actual food-cost percentage* will differ from unit to unit within the same chain, even if purchase prices paid and menu prices charged are identical. In fact, food cost will differ even if we assume that waste, theft, and portioning are held constant. The reason for that is the *menu-sales mixes* for the different units are not identical. I don't know of any instances in which two restaurants sold exactly the same number of menu items. Usually, one will generate more breakfast volume than another, and that in itself will alter the food cost. Typically, breakfast items run lower food-cost percentages than those at lunch and dinner. Therefore, the food cost must be calculated on the menu-sales mix.

The third perspective is referred to as *potential food-cost percentage*. It is also called theoretical food cost because it is calculated by dividing the total or potential food cost by the total or potential food sales. The respective menu price and raw-food cost of each menu item is multiplied by the number sold and totaled. PFC assumes that there was perfect portioning, zero waste, and that the full menu price was received for every item that left the kitchen; thus the designation as *potential* food cost. That's another reason it is referred to as theoretical — it is not realistic. Where the MFC reflects the high-water mark, PFC would be the low-water mark. If everything were perfect, that is the food cost that the restaurant should run.

However, we know that not all the food that is consumed is sold. We have waste, employee meals, theft, spoilage, and discounted or complimentary food items for which no sales revenue is received. And the consumption of food items for which no revenue is received will increase the cost of food consumed. Part of that food expense is a mandated allowance set by management and ownership—employee meals, discounts, or complimentary meals are examples. One must calculate that cost in order to keep it separate from waste and theft losses.

The fourth and final face of food cost answers the management question, "What should my food cost be at the end of the accounting period?" That percentage is referred to as the *standard food-cost percentage*, or SFC. The SFC is compared with AFC to assess the effectiveness of food-cost control during the accounting period. It is calculated by adding employee meals, discounts, and complimentary meals, and management allowances for unavoidable waste and quality control to the PFC percentage.

The four faces of food cost represent the highest food cost can rise and still return a minimum profit; what food-cost percentage the operation actually incurred; the food-cost percentage based on the menu-sales mix and zero waste; and what the food cost should be, given all known allowances for food consumed but not sold. Only then can you fully comprehend the true purpose and value of food-cost analysis.

(1) Setting a standard food-cost percentage can be accomplished by using an industry average.

    A. True
    B. False

(2) The only expense left out of a pro-forma budget is:

    A. Labor cost
    B. Food cost
    C. Payroll

(3) The actual food-cost percentage is calculated by:

    A. Dividing food cost by food sales
    B. Dividing food sales by cost of food consumed
    C. Multiplying food cost by food sales

(4) The potential food-cost percentage is also known as:

    A. Standard food cost
    B. Maximum allowable food cost
    C. Theoretical food cost

(5) The standard food-cost percentage is compared with the actual food cost to assess the effectiveness of food-cost control.

    A. True
    B. False

ANSWERS: 1: B, 2: B, 3: A, 4: C, 5: A

You must forecast accurately how much you are going to sell

ADVANCE PLANNING is an important step in any business strategy. Being able to predict within 5 percent of what you are going to sell can improve the quality of your decisions significantly. When it comes to food-cost control, It's necessary to estimate what and how much you are going to sell of each item listed on the menu. You don't want to run out of something, and you don't want to be left with excessive leftovers and waste.

Knowing what you're going to sell enables you to be better prepared. Armed with an estimate of the number of covers to be served, your sales-mix sales history is used to forecast how many of each menu item is likely to be sold. You then base the purchase and preparation forecast on those numbers so that you do not run out of an item in the middle of a meal

> **"Delegating means letting others become the experts, and hence the best."**
>
> — TIMOTHY FIRNSTAHL

period. At the same time the process will keep you from preparing too much and finishing the day with too many leftovers that cannot be sold a second day.

Remember: Being forced to work with leftovers will result in higher food costs and impose restrictions on your menu offerings. (See *25 Keys to Profitable Success: Cost Controls* for details). Early run-outs not only disappoint customers but can also disrupt the smooth production on the cooking line because demand may switch to a station that is not prepared for the additional volume.

Your chef or kitchen-production manager will determine the amount of food to prepare based on the projected number of customers that are expected at a particular time of day or day of the week. Employees must be scheduled according to the number of customers expected. If you forecast 800 covers for the dinner-meal period, and your menu contains eight appetizers, 10 side dishes, six salads, three soups, 25 entrées, six vegetables, four starches, and eight desserts, you must estimate how many of each you will sell.

If your forecasts are off by more than 5 percent, note your actual sales and adjust upward or downward in the future. There may be valid reasons why your forecast was inaccurate, and such variables should be recorded in your sales history records. For example, your customer count might have been impacted by the weather, special events taking place in your market area, the opening of a competitor, road construction, and so on. If those things can be foreseen, appropriate adjustments in your forecasts can be made. While that method isn't perfect, it's much more accurate than trying to remember what happened last year on Easter Sunday, Mother's Day, New Year's Eve, or the first Tuesday in April. Managers and chefs come and go, so you must have permanent written sales-history records to refer to if you expect your forecasting to be accurate.

(1) To improve the decision-making process, an operator should be able to predict sales within _____ percent.

    A. 1
    B. 5
    C. 10

(2) Working with leftovers will reduce your food cost.

    A. True
    B. False

(3) To determine the amount of food to prepare, a chef must know:

    A. The number of employees in the dining room
    B. The cost of food consumed
    C. The projected number of guests expected

(4) Employees must be scheduled according to the number of guests expected.

    A. True
    B. False

(5) Having a permanent written sales-history record is not important.

    A. True
    B. False

ANSWERS: 1: 5, 2: B, 3: C, 4: A, 5: B

Purchase and prepare according to your menu-sales forecast

HOW DO YOU ACCURATELY PREDICT what you are likely to sell? Every operation needs to conduct a menu-sales analysis. In order to make accurate estimates or forecasts of business volume and menu-item popularity, you must study what has occurred in the past. That means that you must record the sales history for each day. Your past sales records are indicators of what your customers like best and are your best gauge for measuring menu-item popularity. The key is being able to estimate accurately the number of covers you are likely to serve. Most restaurants will retain daily records of their customer counts and have point-of-sale registers that can tally the number sold of each item ordered from the kitchen.

In operations employing a duplicate-check system, the information must be transferred manually from each guest check. Remember: Each transaction must be recorded and entered into your records for effective cost control. If food can be requisitioned from the kitchen without being entered on a guest check or in the point-of-sale system, the transaction cannot be audited. You must have a record of how many of each item you are selling to be able to detect waste and theft. If you know how much you purchased and how much remains in inventory, the difference should be what you sold. Sales records are your basis for control.

A sales history can be kept in an ordinary accounting journal. For each day of the week, indicate the sales for each meal period and customer counts. Keep week-to-date, month-to-date, and year-to-date sales figures. They can be compared quickly with the same day, week, and month figures of the previous year. The menu-sales-mix analysis should be taken at least four times a year if you don't have a point-of-sale system to do it for you. With point-of-sale registers, the information is there to compile your sales history at least once a month and weekly, if desired. When new menu items are added to the menu, their sales will impact other items on the menu. Menu-sales-mix analysis allows you to identify the popular and unpopular menu items and improve the accuracy of your sales forecasts.

You must maintain portion control to achieve standard yields

FOLLOWING STANDARDIZED purchase specifications and recipes won't result in achieving your food cost unless portion standards are followed. Assume that a one-gallon batch of chili has a total recipe cost of $10.00. If the recipe yields 16 eight-ounce bowls, the food cost per bowl will be approximately 63 cents. If the actual yield is only 14 bowls, the cost per bowl increases to over 71 cents. If the menu price is $1.60, we expect to return a 40-percent food cost ($.63/$1.60). (The actual food cost will be 39.375 percent because we rounded $1.58 to $1.60.) However, if overportioning causes us to lose two bowls, the food cost will increase to 44.375 percent ($.71/$1.60). We have also lost $3.20 in revenue because we didn't sell two bowls.

Estimating yields cannot be done by just dividing the total number of ounces by the por-

> **❝Nine-tenths of wisdom consists in being wise in time.❞**
>
> — THEODORE ROOSEVELT

tion size. In this case one gallon is equal to 128 ounces, and eight goes into 128 sixteen times. Yields must be estimated realistically based on actual serving conditions in the kitchen, not on some perfect set of circumstances in a controlled test kitchen. In fact, the reason for getting only 14 bowls may not be due entirely to overportioning. If chili is held on a steam table for any length of time, the liquid will evaporate. We can replenish the liquid, but rarely will we get 128 servable ounces out of a gallon. If some is left over at the end of the shift, it may be discarded for quality-control reasons. Even if a half gallon remains at the end of the shift, some portion will be lost in the normal repanning of the leftover quantity. Therefore, yields need to be adjusted downward when you are calculating the raw food cost per portion. If that isn't done, you will invariably undercost each portion.

And don't think you can cover your mistakes by grossly understating your yields — claiming, for example, only 12 eight-ounce bowls from a gallon of chili. If you do that, you must recover the same $25.00 in revenue from only 12 orders instead of 15. That would raise your cost to over 83 cents per bowl and require you to price it at approximately $2.10.

Selling a piece of pie or cheesecake presents another example of the importance of portioning properly. If you cut a pie into seven pieces, sell five, and throw two away because they were cut incorrectly, your profit goes out the window. You don't make any profit until you sell the last two pieces — the first five just cover your cost.

Here are 10 signs that indicate your portioning standards are not being followed or need to be revised. Keep in mind that under-portioning should be monitored too.

(1) Measuring tools aren't being used to portion food.

(2) Standards are lacking for serving bowls, plates, and cups.

(3) Portion markers aren't used to cut pies and cakes.

(4) Customers tell you that portions are either too large or too small.

(5) Too much food is being left on the plates in the bus tubs going into the dish room.

(6) Customers are making frequent trips to the salad bar.

(7) Entrée portions are too large and are discouraging the sale of appetizers and side dishes.

(8) Dessert sales are low.

(9) Customers are requesting many doggie bags too often.

(10) Too many items are left over or used up early in the meal period.

Granted, there are other reasons than improper portioning that will cause your yields to be less than expected. But if you observe more than three of the signs given, it might be worthwhile to investigate further into your portion sizes and portioning procedures.

Control for waste and theft

IT GOES WITHOUT SAYING that waste must be kept to a minimum. But the truth is, you can find both *good waste* and *bad waste* in every restaurant. Bad waste is what could have been eliminated if proper procedures and planning had been followed; it is having to throw away food that should have been sold. For example, we baked off too many potatoes and ended the night with a full sheet pan left unsold. Perhaps only one pan should have been baked off after the dinner rush had begun. Other examples of bad waste are excessive trim on vegetables and meats. I've observed an employee who was peeling onions and cut too deeply into the layers and was throwing away a thick layer of onion that amounted to 5 percent of the total weight. Those are the kinds of waste that can be avoided.

> **"Men who do things without being told draw the most wages."**
>
> — EDWIN H. STUART

A poorly cut top butt can result in fewer top sirloin steaks and more stew meat and hamburger trim than is normal. While the food isn't thrown out, stew meat and hamburger only return a small percentage of the revenue that can be realized from the sale of a top sirloin. Bad waste also results when food is overportioned. If the corned beef sandwich is supposed to have four ounces of corned beef, and the cook used five or six ounces, that corned beef is being wasted.

I know you must be wondering what good waste is. In every quality restaurant you will find what I call "quality control waste." If your operation has high standards for food quality, you occasionally elect to discard food that doesn't meet your quality standards. For example, the chili might have been held on the steam table at too high a temperature and may have been slightly scorched; or the salad lettuce might just have started to turn a little brown around the edges; or the baked potatoes might have been held in the warmer longer than usual. Perhaps some of those quality standards calls are marginal and could go either way. And if you're obsessed with food cost, you probably might try to serve the food and hope that the customer doesn't notice. But that can be a bad strategy. Quality control requires that an operation have waste. In fact, some restaurant administrators become concerned if you don't have "recorded" waste. The credo of quality control is: "When in doubt, throw it out." Never let the customer make that decision for you!

I once had a conversation with one of my teaching colleagues who, like me, owned and operated restaurants. The topic was dealing with customers who complain about the food. He said, "Remember when we didn't have to give away free food when a customer complained?" These days, we both agreed, you can't charge a customer for something he or she didn't enjoy. But if that is the accepted response to a customer's complaint, how does an operator become comfortable giving away for free what he is in business to sell? The answer was provided by my brother and restaurant partner, who said, "We build the cost of 'quality control' into our menu prices."

I thought that was a brilliant solution. Quality control is good waste. Let's say that such waste will amount to 0.5 percent of food sales. Therefore, if our average check per entrée is $13.95, we would simply add about six or seven cents to our plate cost prior to marking it up for sale. If we're targeting a 40-percent food-cost average, that would raise the price of each item by 17 cents. Now, we can feel comfortable empowering the servers to make adjustments on a guest's bill. Another way to build in a cost factor for good waste is by calculating portion costs at 98 percent of the recipe yield instead of

100 percent. By doing that, we build in an allowance for portioning errors, short-term price increases in ingredients as well as quality control. A "quality" restaurant will always have good waste.

As for theft, prevention is the best strategy. There are so many ways customers, employees, and purveyors can steal from us that it would take volumes and volumes just to list them. You must adopt a prevention strategy and institute controls that will make it difficult for anyone to steal and go undetected. That is discussed in the next tip.

Before you can correct a problem with your food cost, you first must be able to detect that you have a problem

SOMETIMES WE HAVE TO BE KNOCKED on the head to come to the realization that we have a problem with waste and inefficiency. Many restaurants get into trouble because they're wasting time and money. Why has the waste continued to the point where it threatens the profitability of the restaurant? The reason is that management isn't aware that it has a problem until it is felt in the pocket. Nobody can detect the amount of waste if there are no cost standards to compare with the actual results.

Until you discover that something is missing, you might never suspect that theft is occurring. You have to be able to detect missing guest checks to suspect that customers may be walking out without paying, or that one of your servers may be pocketing the receipts. You take cash register readings so you know how much

> **"He is most free from danger, who, even when safe, is on his guard."**
>
> — PUBLILIUS SYRUS

money should be in the drawer and detect whether there is a cash shortage or overage.

One independent operator told me that all of his employees were honest, and that he or a member of his family was present in the restaurant during operating hours. He said he never had a problem with theft. My comment to him was, "How can you be sure if you don't have any way of checking?" He replied, "Oh, I would know." Well I guess that the old saying, "ignorance is bliss" is probably true. But to prove my point that his perceptions could be wrong, we conducted a little test.

His restaurant was well known for its homemade pies, so we decided to count the pieces of pie on hand before and after the lunch period — without letting the employees know what we were doing. We then tallied the number of pieces of pie sold from the guest checks and compared that number with our inventory. To his surprise he was missing 10 pieces of pie. Each pie had been cut into seven slices and sold for $1.95 a slice, so the restaurant was short $19.50 in sales.

That sparked the interest of the owner, and an investigation ensued. He discovered that in the lunch-hour rush, the servers sometimes forgot to write down the pie on the guest check, and the customers either didn't notice or never brought it to their attention when they paid their check. In the process of the investigation, he also discovered that the number of beverages charged on the check — coffee, tea, or soft drinks — often did not equal the number of customers listed. Because he worked the cash register during lunch, he started to ask customers if they had had anything to drink with their food when he didn't see a drink written on their check. What he discovered was that drinks also were omitted accidentally in the same way the pie had been left off some checks. It was an unintentional, but costly, oversight on the part of the servers.

We solved the problem quickly and at no cost. We held a meeting with the servers and pointed out that they were not charging for some desserts and beverages. That was not only bad for the restaurant, we said, but also bad for their tips. Because most customers tip 15 percent of their check, a piece of pie and beverage subtracted almost $3 from the bill. To eliminate those oversights, we required the servers to account for desserts and beverages for the number of customers in the party. For every customer not ordering a beverage or dessert, they were to write "NB" for no beverage and "ND" for no dessert. For example, if four guests were in the party, and three ordered beverages — a coffee, iced tea, and Coke — the check would contain "one NB." If no one ordered dessert, the server would write "four ND." If they could remember to write "NB" or "ND," they would remember to charge for the desserts and beverages. It was surprising how dessert sales increased just because each server specifically asked customers if they would like to try some of their famous homemade pie. The point of this story is that because the owner never looked, he never realized he had a problem.

Calculate your own food-cost percentage. Don't try to use industry averages or another operation's food cost

HOW ONE ARRIVES AT THE TARGET or desired food-cost standard is the most important part of the process. You cannot just pick a food cost at random or apply a general industry average. The food cost your operation must achieve is determined by your operation's financial idiosyncrasies and profit objectives. Your operation's food-cost objective must be based on your prices and operating expenses.

Even within a multiunit chain operation, the costs of land, construction, labor, taxes, and insurance will vary several percentage points. That often will alter the pricing strategy to achieve profit objectives. If the cost of the building and land at one location is $300,000 greater than that of another, prices must reflect the higher overhead of that location.

Franchisees of national chain operations

> **"No more prizes for predicting rain. Prizes only for building arks."**
>
> — ANONYMOUS

find it necessary to adjust pricing of identical items at different locations in the same city or metropolitan area. Have you ever noticed that the prices at McDonald's and Wendy's are sometimes 5 cents to 10 cents higher in commercial business districts than in residential areas? Part of the reason is that the occupancy costs are higher in downtown areas, and the chains have to pay higher wages to their employees to come downtown. Those higher costs have to be recovered by charging higher prices.

When one of your restaurant colleagues tells you his food-cost percentage, consider that he might not be calculating that percentage the same way you calculate yours. Consequently, comparing the two percentages is useless. He might be quoting *cost of food sold* and your figure might be *cost of food consumed*. The latter figure will always be a higher percentage than the former. Ask if monthly inventories are taken. If not, their food-cost percentage is only an estimate and could be several percentage points off. You must be certain you are comparing apples to apples.

Industry averages must be interpreted with a great deal of caution. I'm reminded of the newspaper report that stated: "A man drowned in a motel swimming pool that had an average depth of three feet. Unfortunately, he fell in the eight-foot end." The average of one and 100 is 50.5. The average does not give you an accurate picture of the actual numbers that returned that average. Statisticians know the limitations of the "mean" or average. That is why they also use other statistical measures, such as the median or mode, and report the range and number of responses they collected. So don't read too much into industry averages or those of your competitors.

The food cost that returns the required profit can differ by as much as 8 percent to 10 percent. An operation can be profitable with a 50-percent food cost and be unprofitable with a 35-percent food cost. A case in point: My alma mater, Florida State, used to host an annual industry-recognition program called "Salute au Restaurateur." Part of the program was called "Share Your Success." The respective honorees from state associations across the country would tell the audience their success secrets.

The honoree from a southeastern state was a sweet, elderly lady who had been operating a country buffet for more than 25 years. She told us that she used only fresh fruits and vegetables, and on any given day customers could select from over a dozen different vegetables and pies. Her prices were $3.25 for lunch and $4.50 for dinner, and it was all-you-can-eat. The gentleman that preceded her that morning had emphasized how important marketing and controlling food cost was, and she shocked the audience by telling us that she didn't know about that aspect of her business, but she suspected that her food cost was close to 50 percent.

Knowing what she served and how much she charged, she was probably pretty accurate. I was sitting next to one of my students, and he leaned over and asked me, "How can she be making money with a food cost of 50 percent?" I encouraged him to ask her, "What is your operating overhead and debt-service for your establishment?" Her response provided the answer to his question. She said she owed no one and owned the building she occupied. Typically, one can expect overhead and debt service to run at least 8 percent to 12 percent of sales. She passed on the savings — and additional profit — to her customers in the form of top-quality food, oversized portions, and low prices.

If she sold the business the next week, the new owner could not expect to earn the same profit without raising prices because of the added monthly mortgage and loan payments. Remember: An operation's unique financial idiosyncrasies must be accounted for before a specific food-cost target can be determined.

If you concentrate on selling only menu items with low food costs, your overall sales revenue will not be optimized

YOU SHOULD NOT BECOME preoccupied with low food cost as a single goal of your cost control. For years food cost was the only thing that operators considered important. Consequently, they concentrated their efforts on selling items with low food costs. Low food-cost items are those preparations containing such less-expensive ingredients as chicken and pasta. Breakfast items like eggs and pancakes also carry a relatively low food-cost-to-menu-price ratio.

However, the strategy to sell primarily low food-cost items results in a trade-off: Overall revenue will not be optimized. Consider the menu prices of the items on your menu that carry the lowest food-cost percentages. They probably sell for an amount that is less than your average check. In fact, your average check may be lower than you would like because your menu features such items. If your average check is lowered and you don't increase the number of customers served, your overall sales revenue will not be optimized.

Promoting low food-cost items can result in increased revenue if it attracts more customers to your operation. If your average customer count increases by 25 percent when your check average decreases by 10 percent, your sales and profits will rise. In fact, that is what must happen if you decide to offer discount coupons; if you generate less profit per transaction, you will need more transactions to compensate for the discount. If you don't do more business, though, the discount should be discontinued.

Basically, overreliance on low food-cost menu items will result in lower check averages, and unless customer counts increase, your overall sales revenue will not be optimized. However, food cost is an element that must be monitored — you don't want it to approach the *maximum allowable food-cost percentage* discussed back in key number one. Remember: The MFC is the high-water mark for food cost; if it is exceeded, profit will be reduced. However, we must balance the menu-sales mix to optimize revenue relative to achieving a lower food-cost percentage.

If you concentrate on selling only menu items with high individual gross profits, your overall food-cost percentage will increase and reduce your profit

OPERATORS WHO UNDERSTAND the downside of selling low food-cost menu items often attempt to increase their overall sales revenue by promoting menu items with higher menu prices like steaks and seafood. In some cases the prices are twice that of the low food-cost items. The objective of that sales strategy is to put more dollars into the cash register. But a strategy that completely ignores food cost and concentrates only on the gross profit (the difference between the menu price and the food cost) has a downside. The higher-priced/higher-gross-profit steaks and seafood items also have some of the highest food costs of all menu items. In some cases the food-cost percentage for such ingredients can be 20-percent more than that of the lowest food-cost items. For example, compare a $7.95 pasta dish with a food cost of 26 percent with a $15.95 seafood dish with a food cost of 46 percent.

If your *standard food cost* is 40 percent, then selling items with food costs greater than 40 percent will increase your overall food cost. And there are other drawbacks to having a preoccupation with high gross-profit items besides higher food costs. In highly competitive markets where price elasticity exists, a strategy that concentrates on selling the higher-priced menu items actually may result in lower customer counts. If that occurs, sales won't rise enough to offset the hike in food cost and profits won't increase. If the sales increase reduces fixed-cost percentages more than food cost increases, then profit percentage will improve.

A strategy that emphasizes gross profit for food cost will be effective in operations where price inelasticity exists. Typically, that is in the high-end, white-tablecloth restaurants, country and city clubs, and resorts. It's not an effective strategy in suburban or neighborhood restaurants where many alternative restaurant choices can be found. Consequently, a strategy that seeks to merchandise menu items that have both a high gross profit and low food cost is a more practical approach. That is explained in the next key.

10

Promote menu items that are both low in food cost and high in gross profit

THERE IS AN ALTERNATIVE to having to choose between high gross-profit/high food-cost menu items and low food cost/low gross-profit menu items. Low food cost and high gross profit are not mutually exclusive attributes. Several menu items can help lower food cost and improve gross profit.

Every restaurant operation should have three or four menu items it prepares better than any other restaurant in the area or items that cannot be purchased elsewhere. Those items are referred to as *signature foods* and are the closest thing to a monopoly that any restaurant can have. You can price those items to return a low food cost and high gross profit.

Unfortunately, no operation can sustain a price or product monopoly. Eventually, the competition will respond with a similar item.

And for that reason you must change your menu with regular frequency, which will allow you to find those new signature foods that deliver high gross profits and lower food cost.

One example of a signature dish I featured in my restaurant was spaghettini pasta with a sauce of olive oil, butter, and garlic. We called it Pasta Aglio e Olio. It had a food cost of less than 20 percent and was one of the higher-priced pasta dishes; consequently, it returned a high gross profit. It was a specialty item, and those customers who enjoyed it didn't balk at the price. However, keep in mind that there are popular items that return a moderate gross profit and still account for more total gross profit than an unpopular item with a high gross profit.

For example, consider these two items: Item "A" is unpopular but generates a high gross profit; item "B" is popular but has a moderate gross profit. Their respective selling price/food cost/gross profit are: Item "A" — $15.95/$7.65/$8.30; item "B" — $9.95/$3.31/ $6.64. Assume further that each day you sell four orders of item "A" and 10 orders of item "B." The total gross profit returned from "A" is $33.20 ($8.30 x 4), while "B" returns $66.40 ($6.64 x 10).

The important point in the example is that popular menu items with moderate gross profits will generate more dollars of gross profit than unpopular items with high gross profits. In the example above, item "B" also has a food cost of 33.33 percent compared with 48 percent for item "A." Which would you think is easier to sell: A popular item or an unpopular item? I'll take the item that the customers like best.

11

Four standards are necessary for effective food-cost control: standardized purchase specifications, standardized recipes, standardized portions, and standardized yields

CONSISTENCY IS DIFFICULT to achieve in any cost-control program. The hours consumed in developing recipes, locating purveyors who can supply the brands and quality of ingredients you require, establishing portion controls, and determining your plate cost based on *standardized yields* can be wasted if standards are not maintained. Consider today's date and assume you cost out each item on your menu based on the prices you're paying today. Assume further that you have adjusted your costs to reflect the normal seasonal price variations you will experience over the next six to eight months. You have to do those things because the current menu will be used for the next four to six months.

That exemplifies the importance of adhering to standards. The prices you set today must

> **"When your work speaks for itself, don't interrupt."**

> — HENRY J. KAISER

return the gross-profit and food-cost percentages you require to achieve your profit and sales goals in the coming weeks and months. You must account for all of the "known" variances in cost relative to supply and demand. Granted, there will be times when unexpected weather or labor-related factors might cause the prices for foodstuffs to increase beyond what you had planned, and those extra costs must be absorbed. But those kinds of changes in price and supply don't occur in any regular pattern and cannot be predicted. On the other hand there are those normal variances in price and supply that we know exactly when they will occur.

Faced with all of these uncontrollable marketplace inevitabilities, how can we as operators price our menus today so that they can return an adequate food cost and gross profit over the next several months? The answer lies in maintaining our standards. Recipes are formulas for the preparation of menu items that if followed will produce a consistent-tasting product each time. To ensure that this occurs, the recipe might specify particular brands, sizes, grades, or varieties of ingredients. Therefore, we establish *standardized purchase specifications* that must be followed to achieve consistency. We negotiate with suppliers to guarantee that they will be able to supply us with the ingredients we require at an agreed-upon price for a set period of time. That is one way we achieve cost and quality consistency.

When we use the proper ingredients and follow the *standardized recipe* correctly, it should produce a specified amount of product. If we adhere to our *standardized portions*, we should achieve the *standard yield*. It is the number of salable portions we obtain from the *standard yield* that will allow us to recover the cost of preparing that item. If you don't have those four standards, you won't achieve consistency in quality, quantity, and cost.

(1) Which of the following is not a sign that portioning standards may need to be reevaluated?

- A. Large quantities of food being left on plates
- B. Absolutely no food being left on plates
- C. Customers returning to salad bar after entrée has been served
- D. Excessive need for doggie bags
- E. All of the above

(2) All waste in a restaurant is bad.

- A. True
- B. False

(3) A restaurant's food cost should not be based on:

- A. Prices
- B. Operating expenses
- C. The food cost of your competitor down the block

(4) If you decide to promote low food-cost items, you must attract more customers to increase your revenue.

- A. True
- B. False

5) Which of the following standards is not necessary for effective food-cost control?

- A. Purchase specifications
- B. Marketing efficiencies
- C. Yields

ANSWERS: 1: E, 2: B, 3: C, 4: A, 5: B

12

Leftovers virtually can be eliminated with efficient forecasting and controls

MOST MODERATELY PRICED restaurants have what is referred to as a static menu. That means that the menu basically stays the same from day to day, with the exception of seasonal items being added and deleted — for example, fruits and vegetable salads are added in the summer months, while cold-weather foods like hearty stews and chili are offered in the winter. However, unlike a daily cycle menu or market menu to which items are added and deleted on a daily or weekly basis, a static menu contains the same items month after month.

The frequency with which new menu items are introduced depends on one or more of the following factors: the type of restaurant; the capability of the kitchen personnel; competition; the frequency of visits by regular customers; and the number of covers served each

"Don't bunt. Aim out of the park."

— DAVID OGILVY

day. While restaurant operators would like to limit the number of menu items because it makes ordering, preparation, employee training, and cost control easier, aggressive competition and an exacting dining public demand that new menu items be introduced to keep customers coming back.

When a static menu is put out day after day and week after week, a predictable menu-sales mix will result, permitting management to forecast production quantities more accurately. The ability to forecast with accuracy is an absolute necessity in restaurants with a static menu because they don't have any way of utilizing leftovers the next day. A leftover in that context is any previously prepared and unsold menu item that cannot be sold the next day in the same form it was prepared originally.

For example, a leftover baked potato cannot be reheated and sold as a baked potato the next day. It can be peeled and used for scalloped or hash-browned potatoes, but those dishes require additional ingredients and preparation labor. Granted, the utilization of leftovers is preferable to throwing them out and not recovering any cost. But restaurants with a static menu don't have an outlet for such items, nor do they always have kitchen staffs that have the culinary skills to create new items from leftovers.

Therefore, most restaurants with a static menu work diligently to eliminate leftovers completely. One way to achieve that goal is simply to cook to order. That is practical with any item that can be cooked within a maximum of 30 minutes. Some restaurants even seek to offer items that can be prepared within a maximum of 13 minutes.

Items like rotisserie chicken and barbecued ribs obviously cannot be cooked to order. As a result, they are partially cooked and refrigerated and then reheated or finished off when ordered. Unsold ribs or chicken may have a salable life of two or three days, after which time they must be considered a leftover and either discarded or dismantled and used in another dish.

There is nothing wrong with using leftovers when you have an outlet for them. But the fact still remains that the majority of restaurants don't have a way to work off leftovers; therefore, they must eliminate them. When it comes to cooking in advance, whether it is baked potatoes, ribs, chicken, or hamburgers, amounts must be based on the forecasted consumption of those items. One should cook small batches more frequently rather than preparing large batches less frequently. In that way a fresher product is guaranteed, and leftovers will be minimized.

Developments with rapid-cooking broilers, ovens, and griddles make small-batch cooking feasible. Quartz broilers and combination steam and convection ovens can reduce the cooking time to under 15 minutes on some meat items. Steamers and microwave ovens allow foods to be cooked from a fresh, refrigerated, or frozen state in minutes.

Again, keeping accurate records of customer counts and menu item sales will allow for more accurate forecasting of preparation quantities. Moreover, accurate forecasting will not only reduce leftovers, it also will reduce the likelihood of running out of an item before the end of the meal period.

13

You must understand the difference between cost of food sold and cost of food consumed

FOOD CONSUMED is all food that is depleted from inventory for any reason. That includes food thrown away, given away, stolen, wasted, sold, or eaten by employees. Food sold is that portion of food consumed for which revenue was received.

To calculate the cost of food consumed, or CFC, add the beginning inventory to purchases for the month. That will give you the total value of food available for sale. From that figure you subtract the ending inventory to arrive at the CFC. If you're following the *Uniform System of Accounts for Restaurants*, seventh edition, you are deducting the cost of employee meals from that total. However, to arrive at the true cost of food sold, or CFS, you must deduct the value of *all* food that was not sold.

Consider all of the ways food is consumed and for which no revenue — or only partial rev-

"Why not go out on the limb? Isn't that where the fruit is?"

— FRANK SCULLY

enue — is collected. The more food that is consumed but not sold, the higher your food-cost percentage will be. It's important that you distinguish between CFC and CFS; there is a substantial difference in the dollars and percentage of sales. CFC always will be a higher dollar amount and percentage than CFS because it includes all food consumed. If you don't distinguish between the two, you run the risk of drawing inaccurate interpretations regarding your food cost standards, budgets, and forecasts.

CFS gives managers a more complete and accurate assessment of costs and revenues; however, you must calculate both each month. Unsold, consumed food will increase your food cost percentage, and it is necessary to track and record as much of the consumed food as possible. Employee meals are perhaps the most significant use of food that isn't sold. In addition, certain items may be transferred to the bar. They include fruits and vegetables used in drinks, fruit juices, and nonalcoholic mixes; complimentary meals and discounted meals; quality-control waste; and other recorded waste from leftovers, overcooking, and mistakes.

When the value of those food items is deducted from CFC, you arrive at CFS. CFS represents what actually was sold to paying customers. It is necessary to understand what figure is being shown on your monthly income statement, especially when a *standard food cost* is being compared with your *actual food cost*. Once you understand the difference between CFC and CFS, you can better interpret food cost and determine how much food actually is being sold versus food that is wasted, given away, or eaten by employees.

(1) A static menu:

    A. Changes on a daily basis
    B. Is electrifying
    C. Basically stays the same from day to day

(2) The frequency of visits by regular customers should be a factor in determining the frequency with which new menu items are introduced.

    A. True
    B. False

(3) Static menus can easily accommodate leftovers.

    A. True
    B. False

(4) Which factor should not be listed as "food consumed?"

    A. Food that has been thrown away
    B. Food that has been eaten by employees
    C. Food for which revenue was received
    D. All of the above

(5) The most significant use of food that isn't sold is:

    A. Complimentary meals
    B. Fruits and vegetables for the bar
    C. Employee meals

ANSWERS: 1: C, 2: A, 3: B, 4: D, 5: C

A *fiscal inventory must be taken at least every month for cost-control purposes*

I KNOW THERE ARE MANY operators who don't take inventory every month. At the same time they probably don't prepare a monthly income — or profit-and-loss — statement, either. That is something they do only once a year for tax purposes. Consequently, for the remaining 11 months of the year, they are operating in the dark as far as their food costs are concerned. If you don't take a fiscal inventory — counting and extending the value of all unconsumed food in the kitchen, storeroom and dining room — your bottom-line return or loss is misstated. And if you incorporate those inaccurate and incomplete figures into your decision-making process, the conclusions you draw are very likely incorrect.

When I first went to work for a midwestern family restaurant chain back in 1967, I found all

"What helps people helps business."

— LEO BURNETT

---

kinds of inconsistencies in the way they assembled cost data for their five restaurants. Although all restaurants had the same menu and prices, I discovered that they weren't all using the same ingredients and that they were purchasing from different purveyors and paying different prices for the same goods. That was all detected when I had them take a month-end inventory in the middle of the year. Up to that time they had taken a fiscal inventory only every December 31. The owner and president was under the impression that inventory was basically the same each month over the year, which is far from true.

To demonstrate the inaccuracy of that assumption, I asked the following question: "Why would the value of the inventory be different each month of the year, even if each restaurant had the same sales volume, menu-sales mix, menu prices, food costs, and waste factors?" Hint: What day of the week does the month end? The answer is that it changes from month to month. Given that fact, think about how your ordering and delivery schedules differ by day of the week. If the month ends on a Sunday, the inventory will be much lower than it would be if it ended on a Friday when you probably have your walk-ins and storage areas filled.

Remember: Food cost reflects only food that was consumed. If purchased food is still in inventory, it is not an expense, but an asset. Consequently, if you are using purchases as a figure for your food cost on your income statement, you may be overstating your food cost. If you're using an "average inventory" to calculate your cost-of-food consumed, your actual food cost can be more or less than what it is showing, depending on which day of the week the month ends. Therefore, your choices are: Take inventory regularly and know the true cost of food consumed each month, or take it once a year and operate in the dark for 11 months. You cannot afford to wait 11 months to discover that you have a food-cost problem.

(1) A fiscal inventory should be taken at least once a _____ for cost-control purposes.

    A. Week
    B. Month
    C. Quarter

(2) Preparing an annual profit-and-loss statement will give you a good idea of what your food costs are.

    A. True
    B. False

(3) An operation's inventory can be affected by the day of the week on which the month ends.

    A. True
    B. False

(4) Purchased food that is still in inventory is an:

    A. Asset
    B. Expense
    C. Wasting space

(5) Using an "average inventory" to calculate cost-of-food consumed will give you an accurate idea of your actual food cost.

    A. True
    B. False

ANSWERS: 1: B, 2: B, 3: A, 4: A, 5: B

15

Monitor both the back- and front-of-the-house for food-cost problems

TOO OFTEN THE KITCHEN is blamed for high food cost, when in fact the problem may be occurring in the dining room. The reality is that there are hundreds of reasons for high food costs. In the kitchen you must examine your purchasing, receiving, and storage procedures. Paying too high a price for food or purchasing excessive quantities of perishable items will increase your food cost. Theft by delivery persons and failure to check invoices for correct prices, quality, and quantities can lead to higher costs. Improper storage of items might lead to premature spoilage. Excessive trim and waste on meats and vegetables will raise costs as well. There are many other factors related to the activities that take place in the kitchen that must be monitored.

However, the kitchen might not be the culprit; the problem could be originating in the front-of-the-house, after the food leaves the kitchen. Are all foods served from the kitchen recorded on guest checks or point-of-sales computers? Are complimentary and discounted meals monitored and recorded? Does the number of meals served match the number of paying customers? Do food sales match with items sold? Are you confident that add-on items — coffee, iced tea, desserts, etc. — are being included on guest checks? Do you monitor for missing guest checks and underrings?

Many other things could be causing your food costs to be higher than your standard costs occurring outside the kitchen. Remember: Your cost controls are only as strong as your weakest standard.

16

Be aware that your menu's design might be contributing to your cost control problems

YOUR HIGH FOOD COSTS might be inherent in your menu and not have anything to do with what is not being done in the kitchen or dining room. For example, the menu might contain too many items, which can lead to excessive inventories and waste from items that aren't selling. Poor forecasting might be resulting in overpreparation and unsold leftovers, or the sale of high food-cost items might be overshadowing the sales mix of low food-cost items.

Menu items might be improperly priced. Pricing them too high might discourage selection by customers, while pricing too low can sacrifice additional revenue that would lower your food costs. Sometimes the cost of ingredients increases, and there's no way to increase menu prices in the short run. As a result, food costs will be higher until prices are raised or costs return to normal.

Remember: Menu variety isn't just a numbers game. Offering 10 choices of entrées or salads does not in itself equate to variety if five of the choices don't appeal to your clientele. That situation can result in waste from unsold ingredients. Meanwhile, listing too many items on the menu might be contributing to your inability to forecast accurately. Having to carry dozens of items in inventory will raise your food costs. The techniques of turning your menu into a cost-control and marketing tool are discussed in *25 Keys to Profitable Success: Menu Design*.

Keep accurate written cost documentation for each menu item

DO YOU ACTUALLY KNOW how much it really costs to produce each item on your menu? If you can't show it in writing or in your computer's data base, you really don't know. The excuse that your chef or head cook knows is not acceptable, either. As an owner or a manager, you should have access to that information and conduct your own audits to be certain that the records truly reflect the actual costs. That detailed information cannot be kept updated without auditing it every time a major ingredient cost is changed.

If you simply break down your purchases in the major food categories — seafood, meat, poultry, produce, dry goods, dairy, bakery, etc. — you will see where the greatest portion of your food-cost dollar is being spent. If seafood represents 25 percent, produce 22 percent, and meat 17 percent, those purchases should be monitored more closely than, say, dairy at 4 percent. Within each of the major food-purchase categories there will be specific items, such as shrimp, Dungeness crab, beef tenderloins, or rack of lamb, that comprise the bulk of the food purchases. The high-cost items must be monitored on a weekly basis. All menu items containing those key ingredients would be affected if a price change occurs.

If the cost of the principal ingredient increases significantly, prices must be adjusted or the resulting impact on overall food cost will be felt dramatically. You can purchase software programs that automatically adjust your recipe and portion costs whenever the cost of any of the ingredients rises. If the increase in food cost exceeds a management-set threshold, an exception report is generated, alerting management so that it can develop the appropriate response.

Consequently, you can see why standardized recipes must be developed. They serve as the basis for determining the raw-food cost of each menu item. Without such a written record, the true cost of any menu item is left to conjecture. Restaurants with extensive menus will find food-cost control more difficult than with fast-food operations with limited menus. Without written food-cost records, you cannot assess your food costs accurately.

18

Monitor the prices charged by different purveyors for identical items

WHETHER YOU ARE A single-unit or multiple-unit operation, you must monitor the prices charged by your purveyors for identical brands. An examination of Inventory records of five units within the same chain revealed that the same purveyor was charging different prices for the same items to different stores. You can imagine how the managers reacted when they were told that they were paying more than another unit for the same items. Because the five units were located in two neighboring states, different salesmen called on the various store managers. Certain managers were better negotiators than others, and some of the salesmen had known the managers for a long time and, as a result, gave them better prices.

For that reason the purchasing decision was shifted to the corporate office. While the

"A good plan is like a road map: It shows the final destination and usually the best way to get there."

— H. Stanley Judd

---

unit managers were given ordering authority, they were told who to purchase from and what price they could expect to be quoted. All price changes had to come through the corporate office; notification of a unit manager by the purveyor was not considered proper notice.

Your margin of gross profit will be reduced whenever you pay more than the price recorded in your standardized recipe. When you decide to purchase a key ingredient from another purveyor, and you don't check the price you are being charged, your food costs will fluctuate. If you have multiple units all using the same menu and selling at the same prices, you must be able to compare food cost from one unit to another. Purchasing from an approved purveyor at a predetermined price eliminates one of the reasons for cost variances. A unit manager cannot claim that the reason his or her food cost is higher is that certain ingredients cost more.

When I walk into a storeroom and look at the inventory on the shelves, I can get an idea of the consistency of the food cost and product quality in that operation. If I see two or more brands of canned or jar goods, it tells me a number of things. First, the operation is not rotating its stock. While it's not a matter of perishability with most items in dry storage, it might be an indication of what is taking place with perishable items in the walk-in refrigerators. Second, food costs probably are inconsistent because different brands mean different purveyors — hence, different prices. Third, there probably is inconsistency in the taste and quality of the menu items that utilize the ingredient as well. Take mayonnaise, for example. Not all mayonnaise has the same taste, consistency, and quality. If you're using it to make blue cheese dressing, thousand islands, or tartar sauce, using a lower-quality brand could result in complaints from your customers if they detect taste differences.

When two or more purveyors sell the same brand, that's good news for buyers — we can get them bidding against one another for our business and that usually means lower prices. There are certainly some valid reasons why we shouldn't necessarily purchase from the purveyor with the lowest price, and they are discussed in *25 Keys to Profitable Success: Purchasing & Inventory*. However, all things being equal, we should purchase from the purveyor with the best price.

(1) High food cost is always the result of a problem in the kitchen.

    A. True
    B. False

(2) Which of the following is not a result of having too many items on a menu?

    A. Low food cost
    B. Excessive inventories
    C. Waste from items that are not selling

(3) High-cost menus items must be monitored on a _____ basis.

    A. Daily
    B. Weekly
    C. Monthly

(4) All purveyors in a given area will charge the same price for identical items.

    A. True
    B. False

(5) Finding two or more brands of canned or jar goods in the storeroom can tell you that:

    A. Your labor cost is too high
    B. Your storeroom manager has made a
       mistake
    C. Your food cost is probably inconsistent

ANSWERS: 1: B, 2: A, 3: B, 4: B, 5: C

Adhere closely to your standardized recipes

A STANDARDIZED RECIPE has several advantages. It will produce a known quality and quantity of food for a specific operation. It specifies the ingredients to be used — brands, grades, and varieties; the preparation and cooking procedures; the yield and portion size; and in some cases, the equipment, utensils, pots, pans, and even the flat ware required for service. All of those details aid the cooks with their *mise en place*.

But contrary to what you might believe, standardized recipes are not those previously used in other operations or found in cookbooks. "Standardization" refers to recipes that are "customized" to your operation. They might begin with ideas you took from another restaurant or cookbook but then adjusted for your operation's equipment, ingredients, and serving procedures.

Standardized recipes are another cost-control tool for management and the kitchen staff. They assist in training new kitchen personnel and ensure that the consistency of the food will continue, even in the absence or departure of key personnel. When the recipe remains in the head of the chef or cook, the owner and manager have abdicated some of their authority. As an owner-operator, I was not comfortable when my chef was the only person who could prepare the restaurant's signature menu items. If a chef won't provide you, the owner, with written recipes for every item on your menu, you should start looking for a new chef.

Chain operations like Outback, Chili's, T.G.I. Friday's, The Olive Garden, and Applebee's must have consistency in food quality from one unit to another across the country. Whether we visit a unit in Atlanta or one in Nashville, we find consistency in the way the items are prepared and served. That is accomplished with the help of standardized recipes. If all outlets are following the standardized recipe and purchasing the proper ingredients from the approved purveyors, cost consistency is achieved.

If you don't have standardized recipes, or if they're not being followed, you won't have consistency in cost and quality. If the recipes have changed, let your standardized recipes reflect those changes. If you permit deviations from your recipe standards, you will lose both cost and quality consistency.

20

Account for food eaten by employees

ALTHOUGH THE CURRENT Wage and Hour Law does not require employers to furnish meals for employees, it is a common practice in the food-service industry to give employees a free meal when they work a full shift. While employees typically are limited to what management chooses as the meal of the day, some operators will allow them to order from selected items on the regular menu. Still others will give employees a meal allowance equivalent to actual prices on the menu — $4.95, for example. If an employee orders something that is priced above $4.95, he or she must pay part or all of the difference.

Operators who provide free meals or meal allowances for employees are allowed to take a credit against their hourly wage for the "reasonable cost" of the meal provided. What that

> **"Yesterday is a canceled check: Forget it. Tomorrow is a promissory note: Don't count on it. Today is ready cash: Use it!"**
>
> — EDWIN C. BLISS

means is that instead of paying $5.15 per hour for an employee, you would only pay $4.95 per hour — assuming a meal credit of $1.60 per day. In addition, if you give the employee a 30-minute meal break, you don't have to pay them for that half hour, which further reduces labor costs.

If you provide your employees any kind of meal, free or discounted, the quantity they eat can amount to a significant portion of your cost of food consumed. While many operators offer some kind of employee meal benefit, they fail to account for the cost of employee meals when they do the bookkeeping at the end of the month. You should tally the amount of food cost incurred by employees and deduct that amount from your cost of food consumed.

How do you keep track of what employees eat? You must keep some kind of record, whether it is written on the back of their time cards, entered into the point-of-sale system, or written on special employee meal tickets. Regardless of the procedure you use, no food should be allowed to leave the kitchen without some form of audit trail. At the end of the week or accounting period, tally up the cost of the employee meals provided. An educated guess based on some written records is always better than a wild guess based on what one perceives the cost to be.

You will be astonished to discover that employee meals can amount to between 1 percent and 3 percent of your total food consumed. If that amount is not noted, the variances between your actual food cost and standard food cost will be distorted. My advice is to establish some kind of procedure for recording what employees eat and credit that amount to your food cost each month. It's part of the cost of employing a worker and basically is a benefit; hence, it should not be charged against your food cost.

(1) The most effective standardized recipe is one that has been customized to your operation.

    A. True
    B. False

(2) The best way to keep a standardized recipe is to:

    A. Ask your chef to memorize it
    B. Commit it to memory yourself
    C. Write it down

(3) According to the current Wage and Hour Law, operators must furnish meals for their employees.

    A. True
    B. False

(4) Operators who provide free meals or meal allowances are allowed to take credit against their hourly wage for:

    A. $1 an hour
    B. The price of the meal
    C. Reasonable cost of the meal

(5) Employee meals can amount to_____ percent of your total food consumed.

    A. 1–3
    B. 2–4
    C. 10

ANSWERS: 1: A, 2: C, 3: B, 4: C, 5: A

Monitor food items used by the bar

YOUR FOOD COST must be adjusted for any food items that are used by the bar in the sale of alcoholic beverages. That includes not only the fruit and vegetable garnishes but also the juices and mixers, nuts and popcorn, cheese and crackers, and hors d'oeuvre offered free to customers. Think of the hundreds of dollars that are spent each month on oranges, lemons, limes, olives, cherries, celery, orange juice, and sweet and sour mix. If you provide bar patrons with free food, such as hot wings, a cheddar wheel with crackers, or peanuts during pre-dinner hours, and those items are not subtracted from total food consumed, your food cost will be overstated.

Request that your supplier issue separate invoices for items that are ordered expressly for the bar. However, that is not always possible with such items as oranges, lemons, and limes. An internal bookkeeping adjustment must be made to separate charges for the kitchen and bar. In addition, if the kitchen uses certain liqueurs, wines, and beers in the preparation of food items sold in the dining room, the bar must receive credit from their inventory and bar costs. Let your kitchen manager and bar manager know that you're making those adjustment; it will make them more cost conscious too.

22

Make appropriate adjustments to your food cost for discounted and complimentary meals

WHENEVER FOOD AND BEVERAGE is consumed and not sold, an adjustment must be made to your cost of food — or beverage — consumed. That is done for the same reason you adjust for employee meals and food transfers to the bar. When you offer a buy-one-get-one-free promotion, you will consume twice the food cost and receive only half the sales revenue. Depending on the number of customers who receive discounts, your food cost will increase proportionally, while your average check will decrease. See *25 Keys to Profitable Success: Menu Pricing* for more information.

Whenever customers have a complaint about the food or service, the general response today is to not charge them. There is also the issue of quality-control losses, for which management may require a menu item to be

> **"Thank God for competition. When our competitors upset our plans or outdo our designs, they open infinite possibilities of our own work to us."**
>
> — GIL ATKINSON

remade because it was not prepared properly or not served in the prescribed amount of time. Those are examples of food that was consumed but not sold, and some record of those transactions must be made so that adjustments to food cost can be noted.

The costs of the complimentary meals should not be charged against food cost, but because they are expenses, they must be shown on the income statement. You can consider discounted and complimentary meals as more of an advertising expense, while quality-control decisions should be similarly debited to a quality-control or public-relations expense account. The "be my guest" cards distributed by management or the waitstaff are another example of quality-control costs. Because the customer expects such a response, building a quality-control expense into the operating budget relieves the conflict of interest between keeping food cost down and doing whatever is necessary to satisfy an unhappy customer.

Every quality-control decision should be recorded so management can review the circumstances involved and correct any policies or procedures that may be contributing to the problem. In addition, the monitoring of the redeemed coupons is necessary for two reasons. The first is to assess the effectiveness of the discount promotion — for example, how much traffic did the promotion generate? The second is as a cost-control measure that enables management to audit the discounted transactions. That way an operator can be certain that the customer actually received the discount, and that a server or cashier simply did not attach a coupon after collecting the full price from the guest.

(1) It is not necessary to adjust your food cost for food items used at the bar.

    A. True
    B. False

(2) The cost of free bar food, such as hot wings, peanuts, and cheese, should be subtracted from your:

    A. Menu-sales forecast
    B. Fixed expenses
    C. Total food consumed

(3) Whenever a food item is eaten and not sold, an adjustment must be made to your cost of food consumed.

    A. True
    B. False

(4) The cost of a complimentary meal should be:

    A. Charged against food cost
    B. Ignored
    C. Charged to a "special" expense category

(5) Which of the following is not a good reason for monitoring redeemed coupons?

    A. To ensure that they are not reused
    B. To assess the effectiveness of the discount program
    C. To help audit the discounted transactions.
    D. None of the above

ANSWERS: 1: B, 2: C, 3: A, 4: C, 5: D

23

Review your preparation and cooking procedures for sources of food-cost problems

A MANAGER CAN LOOK for several signs that indicate why the food cost may be out of line with the existing standards. Check your trash cans in the vegetable prep area and look for excessive trim in peeling and cutting vegetables. If you're cutting your own steaks and vegetables, find out if you can incorporate the trim or by-products into new production items. If your menu does not permit utilization of usable trim, consider purchasing precut steaks and vegetables. While your "as-purchased" price per pound might be low, the "edible-portion" cost could be higher than what you would pay to purchase it ready-to-use. In addition, you will save on the labor required to process it yourself. On the other hand, relying too much on expensive convenience foods can raise food costs unnecessarily.

"You win only if you aren't afraid to lose."

— Rocky Aoki

Cooking to order and in small batches is the best way to eliminate overpreparation and leftovers that cannot be sold the next day as the same menu item. If the cooks are not provided with guidelines or are not consulting past sales records to guide their production quantities, losses can occur. Underpreparation can have a negative impact on repeat business if it occurs regularly, and customers become annoyed because they cannot order their first choice.

Check the specifications for grades and brands on ingredients. Using more costly brands and varieties whose attributes are masked in the preparation only adds to cost — for example, a recipe for Waldorf salad that calls for Fancy, No. 1 Red Delicious apples when a No. 2 at two-thirds the price would save on cost and not lower the quality. Buying the highest quality available must be tempered with "for the intended use."

Another factor you should examine is the size of your portions. Many operations are offering oversized portions that offer far more food than a normal person can eat. Perhaps that's intentional in many cases where the outcome sought is having people leave with leftovers in a doggie bag. But there are operations in which customers don't want to deal with a doggie bag, as is the case with business lunches or dinners and with conventioneers and tourists. By reducing the portion to a normal size and maintaining the price, savings in food cost can result.

In my restaurant the portion of Chicken Cacciatore was half a chicken. Our purchase specifications were for two-and-a-half-pound fryers without giblets. Most people couldn't eat that much food. So when we were faced with the need for a price increase, rather than raise the price of the dish, we reduced the portion, not to a quarter of a chicken, but to half of a two-and-a-quarter-pound chicken. The customers never noticed a reduction in the portion size.

(1) The best way to eliminate overpreparation and leftovers is:

A. To use expensive convenience foods
B. To cook to order and in small batches
C. Downsize your kitchen staff

(2) It is a good idea to use the costliest ingredients, even when their flavor is masked in the preparation.

A. True
B. False

(3) Purchase specifications should be based on:

A. The best that is available on a given day
B. The items your competitor is buying
C. Standardized recipes

(4) It is always preferable for a purveyor to make a substitute if he is out of the item that has been ordered.

A. True
B. False

(5) Nearly 75 percent of the food-inventory dollar is contained in the:

A. Walk-in refrigerator and freezers
B. Dry storeroom
C. Bar

ANSWERS: 1: B, 2: B, 3: C, 4: B, 5: A

24

Your receiving practices may be contributing to your food-cost problems

THERE ARE TWO PRIMARY REASONS for establishing standard procedures for checking deliveries. The first is to ensure that you get exactly what you ordered, while the second is to make certain you get what you're paying for. Purchase specifications are established based on the standardized recipes you developed for your operation. All of those written specifications are for naught if the person checking the delivery isn't aware of what was ordered. Ask yourself what document the person in charge of receiving uses to check the delivery. In almost every case it is the delivery invoice. While it may be an indication of what the supplier put on the truck, it is not 100-percent accurate in terms of what was ordered.

In many instances the invoice is signed without checking the delivery for accuracy. If

> **"Opportunities are never lost;
> they are taken by others."**
>
> — ANONYMOUS

that happens with any regularity, you can be certain that even with a completely honest delivery person accidental mistakes will occur where items are left on the truck, especially when large quantities of an item are ordered — for example, 50 10-pound boxes of hamburger patties. Who is going to miss two boxes after they have been put into the walk-in?

In some instances a purveyor, unless instructed otherwise by the customer, will substitute a different brand or grade if the item requested is not in stock. The purveyor will leave it up to the operator to refuse the substitution rather than lose the sale and not provide the customer with some form of the item that had been ordered. While that might appear to be a benefit for the customer, it shows a lack of regard for the purchase specifications. When telephoned about the substitution, the salesperson might say that he charged the same or a lower price. But the substituted item might alter the taste and quality of the preparation considerably. Therefore, to ensure that you don't end up compromising food quality or cost, you should establish a clear policy telling your purveyor what to do in the event that he is out of a specified item.

Another weak link in the receiving chain is the absence of a scale to weigh items purchased by the pound. It's amazing how trusting we are of our suppliers when fresh chicken, produce, and other items are delivered packed in uncertified weight containers. We just take their word for it. That's rarely a problem when you purchase from reputable purveyors who would never condone intentional short weights. However, the human element is always there for someone to take advantage of a lapse in controls.

One of my suppliers received a call from a customer who said he saw its brand of ricotta cheese in an ethnic grocery store priced lower than wholesale. The sales manager checked his accounts and found no record of that retail store as being a customer. Moreover, his investigation revealed that no product was missing from his warehouse either. It turned out that one of his delivery drivers sold whatever was left on his truck after the deliveries were finished. Apparently, one or more of his customers were unaware that they were being shorted product.

The time to uncover inconsistencies in deliveries is when they are made, not at some later date. If items are back-ordered, the person in charge of receiving must notify management so that alternative suppliers can be contacted. In addition, if errors are discovered in pricing or merchandise sizes or grades, items might not be accepted and could require a credit memorandum to be issued. Discovering such discrepancies at the time of delivery is critical so that other arrangements can be made.

25

Your storeroom practices may be contributing to your food-cost problems

FEW, IF ANY, RESTAURANTS EMPLOY a full-time storeroom person to put away and issue products. Most operators believe that adequate controls can be generated without the need for such a person. You can still find a steward in the large hotels with multiple food outlets where all deliveries are brought to a central storage area and then are requisitioned by the various restaurant and banquet kitchens. In high-volume commercial restaurants, the majority of the food-cost dollar is spent on items not stored in the dry storeroom. It is the walk-in refrigerators and freezers that hold about 75 percent of the food-inventory dollar.

It's ironic to find the dry storage areas secured with locks while the walk-ins, where the potential for theft is greatest, are left unsecured. In all my years in the business, I don't recall a restaurant having a problem with a missing case of cut green beans or case of Worcestershire sauce. It is the five-pound box of frozen shrimp or lobster tails that cost $25 to $50 that are likely to "walk away."

Locks are always a good idea, but those areas mentioned eventually have to be unlocked. The important element of storage control is to be able to detect signs that something is missing. That requires that all storage areas be kept neat and orderly, which means that everything has its own place. New product is rotated to the back so the older items are used first. Date stamping of items increases the success of rotating the oldest to the front.

Food must be stored properly and held at the proper temperature. Raw foods should be stored beneath cooked foods. They must be in proper containers and covered to prevent evaporation and contamination. Limiting access to storage areas to only authorized personnel will help with control.

It's also important to purchase items in the size containers most suitable for your needs and recipes. While it is a little cheaper to purchase ingredients in bulk, the inconvenience of having to portion out required quantities and maintain open containers in the storeroom negate any cost advantages. I recommend that purchase units be the sizes called for in your standardized recipes. It's easier to open four one-pound boxes of brown sugar than to weigh out four pounds from a 25-pound bag in the storeroom.

An orderly storeroom or walk-in makes taking inventory easier and more efficient. You can see quickly how much is on hand so products can be reordered. One of the signs that management is not keeping adequate control over its food in storage is the "want list." Whenever I see a clip board with a sheet of paper and pencil for employees to write down things that must be ordered, I know that the owner or manager is not in complete control of the purchasing function. That tells me that he or she is not taking inventory on any regular basis.

Inventory must be taken prior to ordering to determine how much you need, whether it is cases of iceberg lettuce or lugs of tomatoes. If a regular inventory procedure is conducted, you know first hand what you need to purchase. If you rely on the want list, invariably items still will be omitted, requiring runs to the grocery store or extra deliveries by your supplier. If that is a regular occurrence in your operation, you will likely be paying higher prices because of the extra deliveries.

DAVE PAVESIC is a former restaurateur who now teaches hospitality administration at the university level. He previously owned and operated two casual-theme Italian restaurants in Orlando, Fla.; served as general manager of operations of a six-unit regional chain in the Midwest, operating four coffee shops, a fine-dining seafood restaurant and one drive-in; and was a college foodservice director. He currently teaches courses on restaurant cost control, financial management, and food production in the Cecil B. Day School of Hospitality Administration at Georgia State University in Atlanta, Ga. He has written numerous articles on menu-sales analysis, labor cost, menu pricing and equipment layout. His two other books are *The Fundamental Principles of Restaurant Cost Control*, Prentice Hall Publishers, 1998, ISBN 0-13-747999-9 and *Menu Pricing and Strategy*, fourth edition, Van Nostrand Reinhold Publishers, 1996, ISBN 0-471-28747-4.